Kingdom Calling

A Field Manual for Believers

Prepared by

Robert F. Wolff

Don Enevoldsen

Earl Clampett

Mark Huey

Drawbaugh Publishing Group
150 Horizon Way
Chambersburg PA 17202

"Books that make a difference."

ISBN 13 TP: 978-1-941746-57-8
ISBN 13 Ebook: 978-1-941746-58-5

For Worldwide Distribution, Printed in the U.S.A.

Endorsements

Kingdom Calling has been written at this time to help awaken and prepare the Bride and align her into God's plans. It is the simplest of manuals and very easy to process, but it has been skillfully written in such a way to both awaken and cause all of us, as God's committed children to go deeper into Kingdom plans and purposes. This booklet is a *must* read!

Grant Berry, Founder, Reconnecting Ministries; Author and Producer, *The Romans 911 Project*

"These four authors have a clear mandate from the Lord to equip God's People with vital revelation concerning the Last Day's move of God. I encourage you to listen to what they are saying."

Jonathan Bernis, CEO & President of Jewish Voice Ministries International

These four authors have prepared a Field Manual to guide believers into the discovery of their God-given passion and calling in life. *Kingdom Calling* is based on faith, prayer, boldly proclaiming God's word and it is aligned with the Lord's strategic purposes for our day. As the church begins to focus intently on the nature of God's kingdom, the call to equip and release disciples into their heavenly destiny and earthly service has never been more needed!

Peter Tsukahira, Co-founding Pastor, Carmel Congregation, Israel

"The Kingdom of God and His Righteousness" must be the chief life objective for anyone eager to be in a genuine relationship with the very King of Righteousness. *KINGDOM CALLING:* A Field Manual for Believers, a brilliantly succinct, directly pointed, heart-warming yet simply worded guide, is a Kingdom-focused manual for all true disciples of Yeshua. Everyone identifying as a follower of Yeshua needs to deliberately apply the Kingdom principles here so boldly printed.

Raymond L. Gannon, Ph.D., Director of Israel's Redemption

This would have been so useful to me when I was first starting out.

Rowena Cross, Vintage Church Malibu

Reaching beyond human connotations of race, culture, gender, and social standing, *KINGDOM CALLING* speaks to the one blood human race. In Christ, the one new man encompasses all men, women, and children of every nation, tongue, and tribe; with a call to seek the Kingdom of God. *KINGDOM CALLING* is shining a light in the darkness. Add this insightful book to your must read list.

Alveda King, Evangelist, Civil Rights for the Unborn

"We all have lenses through which we filter what comes to us from our surroundings, interactions and relationships. These filters help us make decisions - it's called our worldview. For many Christians there are artifacts which remain on these lenses from our prior life experiences which can lead us astray. Jesus calls us to have our "minds transformed" through the word of God. Kingdom Calling does just that: it helps you correct those misconceptions and form a biblical basis for understanding who you are and how you interact with this world as a Jesus follower."

Judge Vance Day, Former President Promise Keepers

Table of Contents

Answering the Kingdom Calling

The Lord God calls us to live lives of Passion. Lives of devoted purpose. Lives that touch the world with the Love of God. Lives that fulfill His destiny. Lives that reach His highest calling. Lives that are pleasing to God. Lives that advance the Kingdom of God.

Although inspired by this vision of life, the question remains: "How do I live my passion?"

This *Kingdom Calling* Field Manual has been assembled to assist you in answering this basic, foundational inquiry. Inside each of us is a pulse-driven, heart-hungering desire to live a life filled with meaning – a life that reflects no less than the Majestic Glory of God.

Anything less robs us of our potential and ultimate purpose for our short stay on this planet.

Everyone with breath longs for the face-to-face encounter with the King of the Universe who welcomes us into eternity with His highest affirmation, "Well done good and faithful servant."

To this end we accompany you through seven foundational steps of maturity that answer God's Kingdom Calling.

We initiate your Field Manual as: 1.) I investigate the Lord's Prayer. 2.) I acknowledge my identity as one with God. 3.) I accept my mantle of leadership. 4.) I welcome my Father's guidance. 5.) I partner with all humanity. 6.) I receive my Spiritual Gifts. 7.) I exalt the glory of the Living God as presented by Our Lord at His Last Supper.

For every category covered, we voice our Kingdom Commitments over our *Kingdom Calling*.

We encourage you to employ the concluding Gifting Survey to commence your *Kingdom Calling*. Simply complete the survey questions to identify My Passion, qualify My Pursuit, and begin My

Portion. This will fully prepare you to construct your launchpad for a fresh season of dedicated impact alongside other believers of like hearts and minds.

Live out the life you are called out to live. Be equipped. Be commissioned. Be released.

Time to get started. Don't rush. Deep calls unto deep.

The Kingdom of God is at hand; Our King is calling.

Luke 11:1-4

Kingdom Calling to Pray

When the apostles ask Jesus/Yeshua how to pray, He sets the pattern in what's called The Lord's Prayer, for communicating with our Father. The Lord points to our responsibility to release His Kingdom purposes on earth.

The Lord's Person

Our Father

Jesus/Yeshua, the Son of God, addresses His Father as "Our" Father. All humanity shares the same heavenly Father and Creator. We His children are united as one in His family.

The Lord's Principality

Who art in heaven,

Heaven is the dominion where Our Father governs His Creation. Heaven is the realm of the fulfilled, covenantal relationship between God and His Children.

The Lord's Priority

Hallowed be thy Name.

God is holy and His Name is Holy. There are no other gods before Him. There is no one higher. His very Name identifies Him as Our Sacred Lord. In gratitude for His boundless love, we give Him honor and praise.

The Lord's Presence

Thy Kingdom come,

We confidently declare our Father who dwells in Majestic Glory, the One who is, who was, and who forever will be, brings His Kingdom Omnipresence to fill His Creation.

The Lord's Power

Thy will be done

God's conquering Kingdom power is established and His absolute supremacy is demonstrated. Our Lord's Omnipotent Spirit pours out His righteous justice and mercy over all Creation.

The Lord's Purpose

On Earth

Our Omniscient Overseer releases His Kingdom purposes over Earth the Dwelling Place Our Father gave us.

The Lord's Pattern

As It Is in Heaven.

As an extension of His Heavenly Kingdom, a perfect reflection of His perfect plan of divine sovereignty. To accomplish His sovereign plans here, as He accomplishes them in Heaven.

Kingdom Commitments

1. I am a child of God. He is my heavenly Father. We have a loving, family relationship.

2. I am a citizen of heaven. My fulfilled, covenantal relationship with God's person, power, and dominion flows through me as His Holy Spirit draws me closer to Himself.

3. I am standing in the presence of Holy God. My life's highest priority is to bring honor and praise to the One whose Name carries absolute authority over all Creation.

4. I am submitted to God's rule and reign over His Kingdom. My worship is an expression of my acceptance, appreciation and awe for all He is and all He has done.

5. I am obedient to my God's sovereign government to establish His will over all Creation.

6. I am committed to manifesting heaven's purposes on earth.

7. I am dedicated to living my life as an heir of the Kingdom of God by reflecting heaven's Majestic Glory.

Kingdom Calling to Pursue

Having prayed about who God is, Jesus/Yeshua expects pursuit of fulfilled, passionate lives.

The Lord's Provision

Give us this day

Jesus/Yeshua asks Our Father to provide for our immediate needs. His generous hand grants new mercies every morning.

The Lord's Portion

Our Daily Bread.

Our Messiah is the Bread of Life. He is God's Gracious Gift; His Firstfruit that gratifies our every yearning. He Himself is all the nourishment we will ever need.

The Lord's Process

And forgive us our trespasses,

Jesus/Yeshua teaches us to ask forgiveness for our sin of disobedience. We recognize our dependence on God to help us overcome the problems we cause.

The Lord's Pardon

As we forgive those who trespass against us.

Just as we are forgiven, we forgive the sins committed against us, intended or unintended. We give the same redeeming gift of grace that we have received, as heaven's highest and humanity's humblest act of unconditional love.

The Lord's Pathway

And lead us not into temptation,

We align with Our Father's instructions to walk in purity. In following the Holy Spirit's leading we avoid our adversary's tempting tactics.

The Lord's Protection

But deliver us from evil.

Our Savior lifts the enemy's curse, so that none would perish. We enjoy the blessings of peace and freedom flowing from Our Father's Heart.

The Lord's Praise

For Thine is the Kingdom, and the Power, and the Glory Forever.

Jesus/Yeshua worships Father God's Dominion, Strength, and Everlasting Splendor.

> *Our Father sends His Son,*
> *who sends His Spirit, who sends us.*

Kingdom Commitments

1. I am grateful my Heavenly Father continually grants everything I need and He desires.

2. I am rejoicing in the knowledge that God's provision is ever-sufficient and never-ending.

3. I am overwhelmed by God's willingness to forgive me for all that I have done wrong.

4. I am humbled by God's grace to forgive me and I extend this grace to others.

5. I am relying on God's Spirit to truthfully lead me from all oppressive plots and ploys.

6. I am delivered by Almighty God, who protects me from the enemy's curses and schemes.

7. I am safe because my Sovereign God is all powerful. I praise the One who invites me to enjoy a glorious eternity with Him in the Kingdom of God.

Kingdom Calling to Represent Him

Spiritual DNA

We find the key to understanding our identity by returning to the creation of our spiritual DNA. Let's revisit the reason God created mankind. *'Adam* (Hebrew word representing both male and female humanity), is a creation distinct from everything that God had made before.

Image and Likeness

Chapter 1 of Genesis succinctly encapsulates God's purpose for mankind. Verses 26-28 state, "Let us make man in our image, after our likeness, so that they may rule." "Likeness"—*tselem* in Hebrew—indicates a vertical relationship as we stand before God as worshipers and take on His character. "Image"—*demuth* in Hebrew—designates a horizontal relationship as we open our arms to the world, becoming the visible image of the Lord. God verifies His intent for us by granting *'Adam*/humanity dominion over all the earth.

Co-Regent and Representative

Therefore, every believer has been created to act as God's co-regent and representative on earth. We establish the perceptible manifestation of His Kingdom whatever we do, wherever we go, whenever we appear, however we stand. This is why we give all glory to God!

Citizens of the Kingdom

God invites us to be an active, life-giving re-creation of His pro-active, revitalizing character. God, as King, directs His people. We employ our unique identity and authority to display Our Father's character in the world. We are citizens of the Kingdom of God.

References: Genesis 1:26-28; Psalms 8:5-8, 115:16; 2 Corinthians 5:20; Ephesians 2:6; Revelation 5:10

Kingdom Commitments

1. My purpose on earth is to reflect the glory and the will of God.

2. I am the visible image of God to the world.

3. I am an ambassador, a representative of God the Father.

4. Wherever I place my foot, the Kingdom of God is there.

5. I have the mind of Christ/Messiah.

6. I am designed by my Creator to hear His voice and His direction through the Holy Spirit.

7. I am a citizen of the Kingdom of God with authority to declare and to pray His will.

Kingdom Calling to Lead

Believers are Leaders

Believers are leaders. Every person who claims Jesus/Yeshua is a leader, born again, recipient of the Holy Spirit, filled with the desire to answer our King's God-given calling.

Equipping

As servant leaders, we have the responsibility to be equipped and to equip others for service. As God's emissaries on earth, we are created with our Lord's spiritual DNA—commissioned to be a witness to God's love and a blessing to humanity.

God Has No Laymen

Leadership does not require a lofty position of prominence or authority. Our Father seeks humble, steadfast followers distinguished by both a willingness to help others and a genuine commitment to excellence. Our salvation stands for far more than freedom. God's gift of grace further empowers us to do the works of ministry to inspire and advance His Kingdom authority. God has no laymen.

Leaders in the Kingdom

Every believer is designed to lead. We set the example of godly, obedient lives, worthy of imitation. We take the initiative in bringing relief to those who suffer, acting against oppression, and crushing fear. We display our faith in the righteousness, peace, and joy that come from the indwelling Spirit of God. We are leaders in the Kingdom of God.

References: Ephesians 4:1, Acts 2:4, 4:31, Ephesians 4:12, 2 Timothy 3:17, Genesis 12:2, Galatians 6:10, Ephesians 4:11-13, 1 Corinthians 12:4-11, Romans 8:11, 12:1, 1 Peter 2:11-12, Romans 14:17

Kingdom Commitments

1. I am a leader, born again, and filled with the Holy Spirit.

2. I am equipped to share my faith in the Gospel.

3. I am called to equip fellow believers to walk in the Spirit.

4. I am commissioned to be a blessing to humanity.

5. I am willing to help others in the spirit of excellence.

6. I am living a godly, obedient life.

7. I am taking the initiative as a leader in the Kingdom of God to exhibit righteousness, bring peace, and release joy to those in need.

Kingdom Calling Back to Our Father

The Core Issue

The predominant issue of the kingdom story is: "Who governs and rules the world?" The fallen angelic kingdom believes the Creator should have selected them (not human beings) for this privileged position. The resurrection of the Messiah exposes their lie and proclaims to the world that all Kingdom authority has been correctly and rightfully restored back to mankind.

The Bridge of Blood to Life

Jesus/Yeshua as the second Adam reassures the heavenly hosts above and all humanity below that Father God's covenant with His offspring remains steadfast, incontestable, indestructible. The God of Israel directs us to re-establish intimacy with Him by repenting for our rebellious character and by atoning for our misplaced adoration of this fallen world. Messiah's obedient blood sacrifice is the bridge that reconnects us relationally back to our Father and His covenantal promises of eternal life in Him.

God's Circular Road of Return

This Kingdom story is a circular account of our Heavenly Father restoring the broken personal relationship between Himself and His children. Intimately knowing Father God and the Son whom He sent is Life, eternal life – to be experienced in the here and now, to be laid hold of. Separation from God is death. Through trusting in His Son's resurrection and releasing His Holy Spirit, our Maker skillfully guides His children back to the drafting board of His initially intended blueprint. By reinstating my born-again identity, Father God fulfills His paternal promises of protection and provision for all the members of His original family. This completes God's circular road of return.

Kingdom Goals and Earthly Roles

God's goal for His children is to know His rest. We experience His rest as we allow Father, Son and the Holy Spirit to indwell us – spirit, soul and body. As we become one with the Godhead, we become immersed into the reality of eternal life. Because Messiah victoriously broke down the walls of division, we have been freed to express our unified identity as One New Man. As emissaries to the realm of this mutual inheritance, irrespective of racial, ethnic, or geographic backgrounds, the Word of God instructs Jew and Gentile alike to join forces. We obediently release our Lord's supernatural power to witness, to heal, and to serve. We accept the Father's mantle of delegated authority to rule and reign over the nations of the earth, producing peace and joy for all who hunger and thirst for righteousness. This is the Kingdom of God.

References: Isaiah 14:12-17; Genesis 1:26-28, 12:1-3; John 14:6, 17:3; Matthew 6:9-13; Hebrews 3:14-19, 4: 1-11; John 17:20-23; 1 Timothy 6:12; Ephesians 2:11-22; Revelation 5:9-10; Psalms 2:8; Romans 8:15-17; Revelation 19:11-16

Kingdom Commitments

1. I am rightfully restored to my position of authority by Messiah's resurrection.

2. I am secure that God's covenant with me is forever inseparable.

3. I am repenting for my sinful nature as the sacrificial blood of Yeshua has restored intimacy with my Father.

4. I am accepting God's divine blueprint to be the focus for my life. I accept the guidance of the Holy Spirit in all I think, say, and do.

5. I am holding onto my faith in the supernatural cycle of everlasting life. I accept my inheritance as a member of Messiah's family in the Kingdom of God.

6. I am identified as One New Man — the result of Jesus/Yeshua tearing down walls of separation between Jews and Gentiles.

7. I am God's emissary, appointed to represent the Kingdom of God by demonstrating my Lord's righteousness, holiness, and love with all I meet.

Kingdom Calling to be One New Man

God's Covenant with Israel

Our Father's purpose for Israel is unique but specific. Through the lineage of Abraham, Isaac and Jacob, this seemingly insignificant slave nation was set apart to inform mankind of the God of Israel's plans of salvation for all nations. Despite the sinful errors in the Garden separating humanity from their Creator, God initiated a plan to lovingly redeem and restore humanity to Himself. In the many promises and covenants preserved in the oracles of antiquity, Israel was forged as an instrument as a *"light to the nations."* The resurrection of Jesus/Yeshua, the Word that became flesh, ushered in mankind's reconstituted identity as One New Man.

Collaborative Efforts

Hence, the biblical and historical pattern unfolds of Jews in collaboration with Gentiles fulfilling God's purposes to advance His Kingdom on earth. Examples of this divinely designated partnership are numerous: Moses leads a mixed multitude out of Egypt, then heeds his father-in-law Jethro's advice on corporate management over Israel's tribes; Ruth the Moabite marries Boaz yielding Obed, the father of Jesse, the father of King David; David enlists mighty men from other nations to institute Israel's capitol in Jerusalem; Luke pens his writings in conjunction with Jewish authorities; and 1st century Jewish apostles recruit Roman, Greek, and barbarian believers to carry the Gospel to the world. This prescription for mankind's unity is woven into the parchment of God's word.

One New Humanity

This ultimate joint venture to advance God's Kingdom on earth was made feasible because the dividing wall of partition between Jews and the nations was torn down by the sacrificial death of our Messiah. Now after two millennia, with the prophesied fullness of the Gentiles both quantitatively and qualitatively at hand, the One New Humanity is accomplishing the purposes of God to restore the commonwealth of Israel without limit to race, culture, gender, or standing.

One New Man in the Kingdom

The key to Jesus/Yeshua's final priestly plea to humanity is the manifestation of God's love for His children and our love for Him – best demonstrated by our unselfish, uncompromising love for one another as the true expression of our unity. This gives visible proof to all the world that faithful Jews and joint heirs from the nations can indeed come together as one to accomplish the purposes of our Creator. This is the hour to reinstate what has been stolen as we glorify our King. We are One New Man in the Kingdom of God.

References: Genesis 17:1-10; Romans 3:2; Isaiah 42:6, 49:6; John 1:14; Ephesians 2:12-14; Galatians 3:28; Exodus 12:38, 18:17-24; Ruth 4:13-22; 2 Samuel 23:8-38; Romans 11:11-32; John 17

Kingdom Commitments

1. I am a member of the commonwealth of Israel.

2. I am set apart to advance God's Kingdom on earth.

3. I am to be a "light to the nations."

4. I am unifying and collaborating with believers of all nations.

5. I am tearing down the barrier between the nation of Israel and all other nations.

6. I am partnering in advancing God's Kingdom with all believers.

7. I am One New Man in the Kingdom of God - called to love and unite all believers.

Kingdom Calling to His Gifts

Giving

There is nothing our Father enjoys more than giving good gifts to His children. The Lord delights in seeing us accept them, learn about them, and use them. When exercised, these imparted talents testify to the reality of God's Kingdom. Each divine endowment enables His chosen ones to accomplish the work of ministry, thereby extending the reach and influence of His government.

Receiving

God's gifts come in an extensive array. Some are linked to leadership positions; some expand our insight and discernment; some wield weapons over demonic strongholds; some enhance personal passions. Moreover, these treasures are designated to restore our identities, deliver us from bondages, affirm our callings, and empower us to live abundant, gracious, generous lives.

Transforming

Just as there are many needs, there are ample gifts to overcome every obstacle we encounter. There are gifts for healing and for peace. Joy and kindness are granted. Patience and gentleness are shared. Provision and favor are poured out. These spiritual gifts equip us to exhibit our Father's heart and His Son's prayers to share the faith, hope, and love that liberates and transforms the whole world.

Deploying

Deploying these gifts bears fruit and is proof positive that the Kingdom of God is at hand. As we pursue intimacy and abide with our Father, we bear witness to the tangible outpouring of heaven's realm on earth. In obediently applying these gifts, we acknowledge our Lord's power and authority to restore all things as He adorns His bride for His soon-coming return.

References: Matthew 7:11; Ephesians 4:12; 1 Corinthians 12:1-11; Romans 12:3-8; Galatians 5:22-23; 1 Corinthians 13:13; Mark 1:15; Joel 2:28-32; Revelation 19:5-8; Hebrews 10:25

Kingdom Commitments

1. I am the recipient of God's Spiritual Gifts.

2. I am endowed with Spiritual Gifts to tear down the enemy's strongholds.

3. I am sharing my Spiritual Gifts which flow from the Father, Son and Holy Spirit.

4. I am equipped with an abundance of the Spiritual Gifts for every need.

5. I am applying those Spiritual Gifts that confirm the Kingdom of God is at hand.

6. I am growing closer to my Father God every day as I honor the Spiritual Gifts he gives.

7. I am using God's power and authority to apply His Spiritual Gifts to restore all things.

John 17:20-23

Kingdom Calling to Unify

John chapter 17 describes the Kingdom of God as a relational joining together. Yeshua becomes one with our Creator. Our Father correspondingly indwells His Son. We, as God's children, invite Father, Son and Holy Spirit to take up residence – to embody us, thereby completing the unity of God's divine family.

His Kingdom is first formed internally within us, then expressed outwardly from us. We are transformed into living vessels, containing the indwelling presence of God. As a light to the nations, all experience the glory of the living Lord on full display, confirming the manifestation of the Kingdom of God.

Calling for Prayer

I do not pray for these alone, but also for those who will believe in Me through their word;

Jesus/Yeshua prays for these who are present, as well as for those are not near. "These" represents the Jews who sat and listened to Him in Jerusalem at the Last Supper. "Those" includes all tribes, tongues and nations, who believe the disciples' witness and word.

Calling into God's Family

That they all may be one, as You, Father, are in Me, and I in You;

The desire of God's heart is for everyone to be a member of His family. Close-knit. Intimate. Empathetic. Forgiving. Unified. One in the Father, One in the Son, One in the Holy Spirit.

Calling Our Belief

That they also may be one in Us, that the world may believe that You sent Me.

Knowing the Lord means we know about His person and His purpose for sending His Son. God placed His highest calling — the redemption of humanity — upon the life of Yeshua. Being one with God means we share the same heritage. His highest calling rests upon us.

Calling for God's Gift

And the glory which You gave Me I have given them, that they may be one just as We are one.

God does not compromise His gifts. He gives us His absolute best. He gives us His glory. There is no gift greater than the Majestic Glory that accompanies the very presence of God.

Calling to be Perfect

I in them, and You in Me; that they may be made perfect in one,

The presence of God transforms me. I am perfected in His image. I am a full partner with my Creator. My unity with my Creator perfects my imperfections.

Calling the One God Sent

And that the world may know that You have sent Me.

Everything God does has a higher purpose. The overwhelming reality of God's person being revealed on earth is the definitive proof. All God's promises and covenants have been, are being, and will continue to be fulfilled.

Calling for God's Love of All

And have loved them as You have loved Me.

God's love embodies and exemplifies His Father's heart for His family. God loves us the same way He loves His Son.

Kingdom Commitments

1. I am called to pray for these near and for those far away to believe in God.

2. I am called into everlasting relationship in God's family.

3. I am called to be one with God as a witness of my faith in Messiah Yeshua.

4. I am called to receive and give the glory God gave Yeshua as proof of my unity with Him.

5. I am called to reveal God's perfect love as He and Yeshua invite me to be one with them.

6. I am called to tell the world that Yeshua is the One God sent to be humanity's Messiah.

7. I am called to embody and exemplify God's love for all humanity.

John 17:24-26

Kingdom Calling to Unity

Heeding the call to unify, our response is to stand together as a united family.

Calling to Be with God

Father, I desire that they also whom You gave Me may be with Me where I am,

Jesus/Yeshua requests the unity He cultivated with His disciples to continue. The realm our Lord calls us to is not geographical; this is the Abiding Place of union with God.

Calling for God's Glory

That they may behold My glory which You have given Me;

For us to recognize God's glory, we must pass through the portal of physical limitations into the Spiritual dimension itself. In this Place of intimate relationship, we see our Lord face-to-face.

Calling for God's Acceptance

For You loved Me before the foundation of the world.

Everything we experience was envisioned before God said, "Let there be light!" God's love for the first Adam who fell and the second Adam who rose set into motion His miraculous cycle of abundant life. That course reveals God's marvelous design and love for all His offspring.

Calling to Know God

O righteous Father! The world has not known You, but I have known You; and these have known that You sent Me.

Jesus/Yeshua speaks of His intimacy with His Father as only a Son can testify. He declares the nature of God, the supremacy of His position, and the bond of family. Proof of unity between Father and Son is affirmed and confirmed to His disciples.

Calling to Declare God's Name

And I have declared to them Your name, and will declare it,

God's identity has been, and forever will be, hallowed. I freely share my trust in Him.

Calling for God's Love in Me

That the love with which You loved Me may be in them,

For God so loved the world, that He gave His only begotten Son. This gift demonstrates our eternal relationship with our Heavenly Father and our adoption into the blessings of His family heritage now and forever.

Calling for Yeshua to Live In Me

and I in them.

The Father in the Son. The Son in me. I in them. Unity in love in the Spirit.

Kingdom Commitments

1. I am called to join with God within His Kingdom.

2. I am called to witness the glory of God.

3. I am called as a result of our Father fulfilling His grand design for humanity.

4. I am called to testify of God's righteousness and the reality of Messiah's oneness with our Creator.

5. I am called to declare, and to keep on declaring, God's name and authority.

6. I am called to tell the world God's love for Yeshua is the same as His love for me.

7. I am one in the Father through His Son and by His Spirit.

Kingdom Commission

Every believer is called to a higher purpose. Our Lord prepares us by delivering us from sin; affirming us as members of His family; releasing us to advance His Kingdom on earth; authorizing and empowering us to use His Spiritual Gifts to share His Glory as He manifests His Presence.

Our Lord teaches us how to pray. We are cast in His image and transformed into His likeness. We are created to be leaders of nations; ambassadors representing God's Kingdom. Our Messiah leads us back to our Father, who calls us His own. We are One New Man.

For *Kingdom Calling* purposes, the following GIFTING SURVEY will identify MY PASSION and align MY PURSUIT by prioritizing the Spiritual Gifts our Shepherd distributes to His flock.

Awakening to our new identity and accepting our Lord's mantle of authority, we recognize the vital need to embrace His highest call. We have been commissioned by our King.

Now you are able designate MY PORTION to answer your personal *Kingdom Calling*.

The Kingdom of God is At Hand

Our Father sends His Son, who sends His Spirit, who sends us.

Ask yourself two critical questions and fill in your Gifting Survey:

1. What has God called me to do?

   Prioritize MY PASSION (A, B, C).

2. How am I equipped to achieve my heavenly Father's goals?

   Prioritize MY PURSUIT (A, B, C).

3. Identify MY PORTION

Provide a brief answer and date it to secure your commitment. Once the survey is complete, gather with like-minded, committed members of your group to encourage fellow believers to follow their own passions and pursuits.

Name   :

Cell Phone :

Email   :

Address   :

Best Days :

Best Nights :

"For where your treasure is,
there your heart will be also."
[Matthew 6:21]

GIFTING SURVEY

MY PASSION

Which Outreach Choice(s) most closely match my Kingdom Calling? (A, B, C)

Situational

Marriage/Family

Pregnancy

Foster Care/Orphans

Human Trafficking

Recovery/Substance Abuse

Drugs

Alcohol

Sickness

Loss

Needs

Housing

Childcare

Eldercare

Jobs

Other _____

MY PURSUIT

Which gift(s) will help achieve my Outreach Choice for my Kingdom Calling? (A, B, C)

Administrative

Management

Generosity

Recruitment

Marketplace

Directional

Teaching

Coaching

Guidance

Restoration

Hands On

Healthcare

Hospitality

The Arts

Athletics

Other_____

MY PORTION

How am I responding to my Kingdom Calling?

_____

_____

_____

_____

_____

_____

_____

_____

_____

_____

_____

_____

_____

_____

_____

Signature   Date

The Authors

Robert F. Wolff

Majestic Glory Ministries founder Robert Wolff advocates reconciliation between Jews and Gentiles by accepting our God-given identity as One New Man in Messiah Yeshua. His use of *Kingdom Kinetics* employs publishing, speaking and media platforms to achieve unity within the Kingdom of God. Find us: Awakening1.org

Robert previously released: *UNITY: Awakening the One New Man*; *Catch & Release: A Church Set Free*; *Have You Seen the Lamb?*; *Sitting with Seamoor*; and *My First 40 Days with the Lord*.

He coordinates The Many Waters Educational Foundation joining the First Nations of America with the Nation of Israel via mutually beneficial enterprises. His Sign the O.A.T.H. Project (One Against Trafficking Humanity) combats slavery by enlisting both faith and secular communities. He and his wife Wendy reside in Malibu.

Don Enevoldsen

Don Enevoldsen is the founder and director of CounterThought. org, a ministry devoted to challenging church tradition, not with hostility but with a view to assessing the biblical validity and viability of what is taught and lived, with a particular emphasis on abuse in all forms. The foundation of his ministry is the proclamation of the rulership of God through his people, as encapsulated in the Gospel of the Kingdom that Jesus preached.

Don has published numerous works, including *The Wealth of the Wicked*; *Friends, Family & Other Enemies*; *Simple Prayer*; *On These Two Commandments*; and *The Hazards of Forgiveness*. He currently works with The Family Offices, a ministry devoted to fostering healthy marriages and families. He and his wife Christina reside in Phoenix, Arizona.

Earl Clampett

Earl Clampett is a retired attorney, Admin. Law Judge and Jail Chaplain with the San Diego County Sheriff Dept. He is an ordained minister with a B.A. Degree in Theology, Magna Cum Laude, from Life Bible College. He has authored 2 books: *God's Got a Problem on His Hands* and *The Blueprint: Is God's Bible Design Linear or Circular?* A third book to be released in 2021 is entitled: *Homecoming: How the New Covenant Brings Both Jew and Gentile back to Abba Father.*

His writings and teachings can be accessed at - Simpletruth ministries.net. He is married with 4 children and 2 grandchildren.

Mark Huey

Mark Huey is the founder and director of Outreach Israel Ministries (outreachisrael.net), a ministry dedicated to helping Believers understand the full and undivided counsel of the Holy Scriptures from Genesis to Revelation. He is teacher, speaker, and the author of several books including: five commentaries on the Torah in the TorahScope series; *Counting the Omer: A Daily Devotional Toward Shavuot; Sayings of the Fathers: A Messianic Perspective on Pirkei Avot*; with contributions to many other books.

Currently, Mark works for the Messianic Jewish Alliance of America, as the Director of Partner Relations for the Joseph Project, a humanitarian aid venture in Israel. He is a Messianic Believer and currently serves as an elder at a Messianic Jewish Congregation in the Dallas area. He resides in the McKinney, Texas area with his wife Margaret, and has five children and three grandchildren.

CPSIA information can be obtained
at www.ICGtesting.com
Printed in the USA
BVHW052341230721
612358BV00005B/22

9 781941 746578